MW00457500

SERMON OUTLINES on

Lay Ministry Opportunities

Also by Al Bryant

SERMON OUTLINES

on

Lay Ministry
Opportunities

compiled by
Al Bryant

kregel
PUBLICATIONS

Grand Rapids, MI 49501

Sermon Outlines on Lay Ministry Opportunities by Al Bryant.

Copyright © 1995 and published by Kregel Publications, a division of Kregel, Inc., P. O. Box 2607, Grand Rapids, MI 49501. Kregel Publications provides trusted, biblical publications for Christian growth and service. Your comments and suggestions are valued.

All rights reserved. No part of this book may be reproduced, stored in a retrieval system, or transmitted in any form or by any means—electronic, mechanical, photocopy, recording, or otherwise—without written permission of the publisher, except for brief quotations in printed reviews.

Library of Congress Cataloging-in-Publication Data
Bryant, Al (1926–
   Sermon outlines for lay leaders / [compiled by] Al Bryant.
     p. cm.
   1. Lay preaching. 2. Sermons—Outlines, syllabi, etc.
I. Bryant, Al, 1926–   .
BV4235.L3S47   1995   252'.02—dc20   95-7843
                                       CIP

ISBN 0-8254-2094-6

2 3 4 5 6 / 07 06 05 04 03

Printed in the United States of America

CONTENTS

Sermons for Soul-Winning

PREFACE

Christian laypeople today have greater opportunities than ever before to participate in mission meetings, evangelistic services and various other secular and church occasions. It is to provide them with suggestions for Bible-centered talks that this collection of sermon outlines and illustrations has been compiled from sources many and varied. The collection is divided into three broad categories:

- Messages for men
- Secrets of Christian living
- Soul-winning sermons

In this book you will find outlines to help you present the claims of the Gospel in evangelistic messages, outlines dealing with the Bible's principles for practical Christian living, and messages for men based upon stories from the lives of Bible men from the Old and New Testaments. It is the compiler's prayer that you will find just the right message among the many outlines in this collection.

Pastors, too, will find these messages extremely useful as a source of ideas for presentation before laymen's groups.

It is my hope and prayer that each outline in this book will be used of God to convict the unsaved of their need of a Savior—and to convince other Christian laypeople of the importance and urgency of a forthright and uncompromising witness.

AL BRYANT

SCRIPTURE INDEX

ANDREW—THE SOUL-WINNER

John 1:40–42; 6:5–11; 12:20–22

I. **Andrew Is Mentioned 13 Times in the Gospels**
   A. He never preached a sermon.
   B. He never wrote a book.
   C. He never held an office.
   D. He was an ordinary man.
   E. The world saw Peter—God saw Andrew.

II. **John Gives 3 Pictures of Andrew**
   A. John 1—his brother, Peter.
   B. John 6—lad, loaves and fishes.
   C. John 12—Greeks.
   D. Andrew had one talent and used it.
   E. Andrew's reward:
      1. He saw 3,000 people won by Peter.
      2. He saw 5,000 people fed.
      3. He saw Greeks find Christ.

III. **Andrew Was a Sower**
   A. He sowed Peter, Peter reaped Pentecost.
   B. Sowing is lonely, hard work.
   C. Sowing is done in the spring, weather raw and wet.
   D. Sowing means plowing and toiling.
   E. Sower's picture is always one person.

IV. **Jesus Gives the Commission in Acts 1:8**
   A. Simon Peter in Judea. Andrew's first concern was his brother (John 1:41). Andrew began at home with hard-to-win loved ones. Andrew picked an unlikely, unpromising prospect, a blunderer, loose-tongued, hot-tempered, cursing, swearing Simon.
   B. Lad in Samaria (John 6:5–11).
   C. Greeks—Gentiles—from uttermost parts.
      Regard of other disciples for Andrew as a personal worker.
      He was not an orator.
      He was not a writer.
      He was not a personality, but a soul-winner.

Selected

THE FISHERMAN WHO WARMED HIS HANDS AT THE WRONG FIRE

Matthew 26:35–75

Introduction

In spite of Peter's backsliding, Jesus loved him (Mark 16:7), because:

I. Peter Has Fallen into a Subtle Trap

A. He was the picture of discouragement.

B. He was overcome by his own inner fear.

C. He was a victim of bewilderment.

D. He was a victim of his own overconfidence.

II. Peter Was Basically Sincere

A. He tried in Gethsemane to defend Jesus.

B. When others fled completely, he followed afar off.

III. Peter Was Unaware of the Subtle Steps in His Spiritual Decline

A. Explanation: Matthew 26:35, 74.

B. In between these verses are the subtle steps in backsliding:

1. Spiritual sleeping (vv. 36–41).

2. Unchristian behavior (vv. 51–52).

3. Followed afar off (vv. 57–58).

4. Associated with wrong crowd (v. 58).

5. Succumbed to social pressure (vv. 69–73).

Les Parrott

BOAZ—A TYPE OF CHRIST

1. **Lord of the harvest.**

2. **Near kinsman.**

3. **Supplier of wants.**

4. **Redeemer of the inheritance.**

5. **Man who gives rest.**

6. **Wealthy kinsman.**

7. **Bridegroom.**

D. L. Moody

THE MINISTRY OF PHILIP

Acts 8:26–39

1. **He Was Obedient to the Divine Command (Acts 8:27).**
   Unlike Jonah he did not run away (Josh. 1:16; Mark 16:15; Acts 8:4–5; 2 Tim. 4:7–8).

2. **He Was Zealous in His Ministry (Acts 8:30).**
   Like Paul—both before and after his conversion (Matt. 23:15; Acts 22:3–5; 2 Cor. 9:6; Gal. 6:9).

3. **He Used Wise Methods of Approach (Acts 8:30).**
   Fishermen must be wise (Matt. 10:16; 1 Cor. 9:19–23; 2 Cor. 5:14; 1 Peter 3:16).

4. **He Was a Simple Gospel Preacher (Acts 8:35).**
   He had no program, only the Great Commission (1 Kings 20:40; Acts 20:25–27; 1 Cor. 9:16; 2 Tim. 4:2, 7).

5. **He Was Able to Gather a Harvest (Acts 8:37).**

C. C. Maple

LESSONS FROM THE LIFE OF LOT

I. What He Did
   A. He looked. "Lot lifted up his eyes" (Gen. 13:10).
   B. He chose. "Chose . . . all the plain" (13:11).
   C. He journeyed. "Lot journeyed east" (13:11).
   D. He pitched. "His tent toward Sodom" (13:12).
   E. He lingered. "While he lingered" (19:16).

II. What He Lost
   A. His testimony. "Seemed as one that mocked" (19:14).
   B. His wife. "A pillar of salt" (19:26).
   C. His communion. No communion in Sodom.
   D. His property. Went in rich, came out poor.
   E. His character. A drunkard (19:35).
   F. Nearly lost his life. Was urged to leave (19:22).

Author Unknown

NEHEMIAH

Nehemiah had seven forms of opposition in his work:

1. **The laughter of the enemy (Neh. 2:19).**
2. **The grief of the enemy (2:10).**
3. **The wrath of the enemy (4:1).**
4. **The mocking of the enemy (4:3).**
5. **The conflict with the enemy (4:8).**
6. **The subtility of the enemy (6:1).**
   By the subtility within (6:10).
7. **By craft without (6:19).**
   Nehemiah began his work in prayer (1:4).
   Nehemiah continued his work in prayer (4:4).
   Nehemiah did not cease at the end of his work. "Remember me, O my God, for good" (13:31).

D. L. Moody

SAMUEL THE SERVANT

1. **The LISTENING servant**
   "Thy servant heareth" (1 Sam. 3:9).
2. **The HUMBLE servant**
   "Opened the doors" (3:15).
3. **The DILIGENT servant**
   "And he answered, Here am I" (3:16).
4. **The FAITHFUL servant**
   "And hid nothing from him" (3:18).
5. **The PROGRESSIVE servant**
   "And Samuel grew" (3:19).
6. **The PRIVILEGED servant**
   "And the Lord was with him" (3:19).
7. **The POWERFUL servant**
   "None of his words fell to the ground" (3:19).
8. **The DISTINGUISHED servant**
   "All Israel . . . knew that Samuel . . ." (3:20).

Author Unknown

SIX THINGS ABOUT THE PRODIGAL SON

Luke 15:11–32

1. His condition—"In want" (v. 14).
2. His conviction—"Came to himself" (v. 17).
3. His confidence—"I will arise" (v. 18).
4. His confession—"I have sinned" (v. 18).
5. His contrition—"No more worthy" (v. 19).
6. His conversion—"He arose and came" (v. 20).

Turning Points in His Life:

1. Sick of home (vv. 12–13).
2. Homesick (vv. 17–19).
3. Home (vv. 20–24).
4. Sequel (vv. 25–32).

Six Cases of Men "Afar Off" from God:

1. The prodigal (15:13).
2. The rich man (16:23).
3. The ten lepers (17:12).
4. The publican (18:13).
5. The beggar (18:40).
6. Peter (22:54).

D. L. Moody

THE BELIEVER

His Salvation—(Hebrews 5:9)
His Preservation—(Jude 1)
His Presentation—(Romans 12:1)
His Proclamation—(2 Timothy 4:2)
His Exclamation—(Zechariah 9:17)
His Occupation—(1 Peter 2:16)
His Consummation—(John 17:24)

Pegs for Preachers

PILATE—THE RULER WHOSE CONSCIENCE DIED

Matthew 27:1–26

Introduction

The greatest single chapter on conscience is Matthew 27.

I. The Tormented Conscience (Matt. 27:1–5)
A. Thirty pieces of conscience money.

II. The Conscience of Convenience (Matt. 27:6–8)
A. Priests collected the thirty pieces which Judas threw down.

B. They piously used it for charity, to buy a potter's field.

III. Enlightened Conscience (Matt. 27:19)
A. Pilate's wife had a sense of moral responsibility.

B. Not a nocturnal experience, but a struggle with conscience.

IV. A Seared Conscience (Matt. 27: 24–26)
Steps to a seared conscience.

A. Conscience awakened (Matt. 27:11–14).

B. Conscience struggling (Matt. 27:15–18).

C. Conscience compromised (Matt. 27:21–23).

D. Conscience seared (Matt. 27:24–26).

Conclusion

Conscience can be a valuable guide to right moral decisions only if it is kept tender, enlightened and based on God's Word.

Les Parrott

ATTITUDE OF THE BELIEVER

Looking—(Heb. 12:2)
Listening—(Ps. 85:8)
Learning—(Matt. 11:29)
Living—(Phil. 1:21)
Lying—(Ps. 23:2)
Loving—(1 John 4:19)
Longing—(Ps. 119:174)

Pegs for Preachers

THE DYING THIEF

Luke 23:42

Introduction

This one brief sentence not only calls for our profound respect, but it describes a moment of unparalleled faith; of true, genuine, saving faith in the Redeemer of mankind; of faith unsurpassed and unexampled. History presents nothing like it; earth had never seen its like before. It was an accepted faith; and, thief though he was, perishing though he was, the dying Savior, whom he was not ashamed to acknowledge as such, pronounced the blessed assurance to him, "This day shalt thou be with me in paradise."

I. True faith is self-condemnatory; it is rooted and grounded in sincere repentance.

II. His faith was also unhesitating, full, confiding.

III. His faith was frank and open.

IV. His faith was spiritual; it looked through and over all mere outward circumstances.

V. The object petitioned for has respect exclusively to the higher interests of a life beyond the grave.

Conclusion

A. The subject before us shows no one need despair.

B. To the Christian, when contemplating an approach to the Lord's table, this subject is rich in instruction and replete with encouragement.

W. T. Hamilton

PRECIOUS P'S

(1 John 3:1–3)

I. Priceless Privilege (verse 1)
II. Positive Promise (verse 2)
III. Purifying Power (verse 3)

Gleanings

MAN WHO PLAYED THE FOOL

1 Samuel 26:21

There are a great many fools mentioned in the Bible. We can't deal with each of them. But those whom we will discuss have special prominence in the eyes of God.

1. The Atheistic Fool

"The fool hath said in his heart, 'There is no God.'"

A fool is one who speaks and acts contrary to reason. The man who declares that there is no God is such a man. One might as well declare that there is no air. One does not debate the presence of air, he merely uses it. The Bible does not try to prove the presence of God. It uses it.

The best science can do is to lead us back to protoplasm and then say, "Evolution." But what is behind the protoplasm? The Bible gives the answer: "In the beginning, God."

2. The Conceited Fool

This is the man who believes in God and yet thinks that he can make a success without Him. He substitutes self for God. This was the sin of which Saul was guilty. His head had been turned by victory. He took full credit for everything himself. Then the disastrous end came. He had played the fool.

A man without God is dead in sins and trespasses. He cannot perform his mission in life without the power of God animating him, controlling him, and making him equal to the task he has to do. Turn on the electricity, and the car moves along the track to perform its mission. Unite your soul through Jesus Christ to God, and His Spirit will come into your life and give you mastery over sin.

3. The Selfish Fool

Jesus describes this fool in Luke 12. He was the man who was successful. He was going to tear down his barns to build greater. He was going to take his ease—eat, drink and be merry. But God said unto him: "This night thy soul will be required of thee. Then whose will these things be?"

4. The Careless Fool

The world is filled with fools like this. They do not prepare for life. While great battles are to be fought they are "fooling around." Every day the crisis of life comes to someone. Are you ready for it to come to you? Have you built the reserves of Christian character so essential for this time?

R. M. Brougher

BEWARE OF PRIDE

I. How Pride Originates
A. Through self-righteousness (Luke 18:11–12).
B. Through inexperience (1 Tim. 3:6).
C. Through a good countenance (Ps. 10:4).
D. Through possessing riches (2 Chron. 32:23–26).

II. What Pride Leads To
A. Contempt of God's Word (Jer. 43:1–2).
B. A persecuting spirit (Ps. 10:2).
C. Conflict (Prov. 13:10).
D. Awful deception (Jer. 49:16).

III. What Pride Is
A. It is hateful to God (Prov. 6:16–17).
B. It is ruinous to man (Prov. 16:18).

IV. What Pride Did
A. Drove our first parents from Eden (Gen. 3:22–24).
B. Slew Saul on Mount Gilboa (1 Sam. 31:4).
C. Banished Nebuchadnezzar from his throne (Dan. 5:18–21).
D. Robbed Belshazzar of his kingdom (Dan. 5:22–30).
E. Hanged Haman on the gallows (Esther 7:10).
F. Cast Lucifer out of heaven (Isa. 14:12–15).

Selected

PETER'S SIN

And the Lord turned and looked upon Peter (Luke 22:61).

The sins of God's people are noted in Scripture to show us first that we must cut off all man-worship in the church of Christ; second, to show us that it was not through works, but entirely through Christ, that even the most eminent and faithful of God's servants were chosen; third, that we may learn to know the evil of the unbelief that is within us, and that we are altogether dependent upon the grace of God.

I. Mark How the Strongest Are Weak in Their Strongest Point.
A. Peter's courage and election were the very points in which he failed.

II. Peter Sinned Against Light—Bright and Fully Revealed Light.
A. Jesus was before him when he denied Him.

B. So do we all sin against light and in the presence of light.

III. Remember How Christ Had Forewarned Peter.
A. He not only saw Peter manifesting his zeal and devotion, but He beheld that awful enemy who was to assail him.

IV. This Looking Showed That While the Eye of Christ Was Resting on the Failings of Peter, It Was Penetrating the Innermost Recesses of His Heart.
A. That look of Jesus, although it was like a sharp sword piercing the very heart of Peter, was also the healing balm, the life-giving tide, the refreshing rain which came into the soul of Peter.

Three Hundred Outlines on the New Testament

THE VICTOR'S CROWN

I will give thee a crown of life (Rev. 2:10)

I. The Christian's reward is glorious—"A crown"

II. The Christian's reward is durable—"A crown of life"

III. The Christian's reward is personal—"I will give Thee"

Pulpit Germs

THE HAPPY AND THE UNHAPPY MAN

Psalm 1:1–6

Two characters are brought before us; the one is pronounced happy, and the other miserable. Three things are said to characterize *the good man*:

I. He Shuns Evil Companions.

A. Here is a classification of the wicked; ungodly, sinners, scornful; that is, without God—opposed to God—and having contempt for God.

B. Here is a graduated scale of depravity—walking, standing, sitting.

II. He Delights in the Word of God.

A. The word "law" here stands for the whole of divine revelation.
1. Show me a holy, God-fearing man, and I will show you one who loves the Bible.
2. And what a man loves he thinks about; and so we read, "In his law he meditates day and night."

III. He Is Like a Tree Planted.

A. He is like a tree in his growth.
1. "Consider the lilies, *how* they grow."
B. "A tree planted"—that is, a tree cared for.
1. Such a tree is fenced in to protect it from wild beasts.
2. It is staked to preserve it from the wind.
3. It is watered in the time of drought.

Three things are affirmed of *the wicked man*:

I. He Will Be Condemned in the Judgment.

A. "Shall not stand in the Judgment."
1. This does not mean that he will not be present; "for we shall all appear before the Judgment Seat of Christ"; but the word "stand" here is a law term, and means the same as to be "justified."

II. His Companionship with the Righteous Will Terminate.

A. "Nor sinners in the congregation of the righteous."

Farewell, holy Sabbaths; farewell, house of God; farewell, praying father and mother!

III. His End Will Be Destruction.

    A. "The way of the ungodly shall perish."

    B. How much that means we do not know, but it is a doom that Jesus wept over, and died to save us from.

Revival Sermons in Outline

THE BELIEVER'S CALLING

I.	**He who calls—**	**God**	**(Rom. 8:28-30)**
II.	**From what He calls—**	**Darkness**	**(1 Peter 2:9)**
		Sonship	**(1 John 3:1)**
		Saints	**(Rom. 1:7)**
		Servants	**(1 Peter 2:16)**
III.	**To what He calls us**	**Unity**	**(Col. 1:9)**
		Fellowship	**(1 Cor. 1:9)**
		Suffering	**(1 Peter 2:21)**
		Kingdom	**(1 Thess. 2:12)**
IV.	**Character of the calling**	**Holy**	**(2 Tim. 1:9)**
		Heavenly	**(Heb. 3:1)**

Pegs for Preachers

DEEPER LIFE

Genesis 32:24–31

1. Solitude. Jacob was left alone (v. 24).

2. Subjection (v. 25).

3. Supplication, "I will not let Thee go except thou bless me" (v. 26).

4. Searching of heart. "What is thy name? And he said, Jacob" (v. 27).

5. Secret of power (with God and men) (v. 28).

6. Security. Our life is preserved (v. 30).

7. Sunshine. "And as He passed over Penuel the sun rose upon him" (v. 31).

Selected

GOOD WORKS

Matthew 5:16

1. To glorify God (Col. 1:10; Titus 1:16).

2. To be a good example (Acts 9:36; Titus 2:7).

3. To please our Lord (Titus 2:14; Heb. 13:16).

4. Always ready to serve (Titus 3:1; 1 Peter 2:12).

5. Not for salvation (Matt. 7:22; Rom. 3:20; Eph. 2:8–9).

6. Good works a daily practice (Titus 3:8; 1 Peter 2:20–22).

7. Rich in good works (Luke 6:35; Gal. 6:10; 1 Tim. 6:18).

8. For inspiration to others (Heb. 10:24).

Selected

TWELVE COMMANDMENTS FOR CHRISTIAN FAMILIES

1. Be not conformed to this world (Rom. 12:2).

2. Be ye followers of God, as dear children (Eph. 6:1).

3. Be ye sober, and watch unto prayer (1 Peter 6:7).

4. Be kindly affectioned one to another (Rom. 12:10).

5. Be content with such things as ye have (Heb. 13:5).

6. Be ye doers of the Word, and not hearers only (James 1:22).

7. Be ye of one mind, live in peace (2 Cor. 8:11).

8. Be patient toward all men (1 Thess. 5:14).

9. Be clothed with humility (1 Peter 5:5).

10. Be sympathetic, be courteous (1 Peter 3:8).

11. Be glad in the Lord, and rejoice (Ps. 32:11).

12. Be ye ready, for the Son of Man cometh (Luke 12:40).

S. R. Briggs

THE RESULTS OF THE NEW BIRTH

1. LIKENESS. "The image of him that created him" (Col. 3:10).

2. KNOWLEDGE. "Renewed in knowledge" (Col. 3:10).

3. HATRED OF SIN. "Doth not commit sin" (1 John 3:9).

4. VICTORY. "Overcometh the world" (1 John 5:4).

5. LOVE TO ALL SAINTS. "We love the brethren" (1 John 3:14).

Author Unknown

GOD IS ABLE

1. Able to Sympathize (Heb. 4:15–16).

2. Able to Succor (Heb. 2:18).

3. Able to Save (Heb. 7:25).

4. Able to Make You Stand (Rom. 14:4).

5. Able to Establish You (Rom. 16:25).

6. Able to Keep You from Falling and to Present You Faultless (Jude 24).

7. Able to Make Grace Abound Toward You (2 Cor. 9:8).

8. Able to Keep (2 Tim. 1:12).

9. Able to Build You Up (Acts 20:32).

10. Able Even to Subdue You (Phil. 3:21).

11. Able to Do Exceedingly Abundantly above All That We Ask or Think (Eph. 3:20).

Author Unknown

THE CHRISTIAN'S PLACE IN THE WORLD

Sent into the World (John 17:18; 20:21)
Preaching to the World (Mark 15:15)
The Light of the World (Phil. 2:15; Matt. 5:14)
Live Godly in the World (Titus 2:12)
Not Conformed to the World (Rom. 12:2; John 17:15)
Love Not the World (1 John 2:16; 2 Tim. 4:10)
Passing through the World (1 Peter 2:11)
No Friendship with the World (James 4:4; 1:27)

500 Bible Subjects

THINGS TO BE EXPECTED IN THE LIFE OF A CHRISTIAN

Hebrews 6:9

1. He Should Live a Life of Spiritual Victory (Gal. 5:22).
Our walk must correspond with our profession (1 Thess. 5:22; 2 Tim. 2:19; Heb. 12:14; 1 John 2:6).

2. He Should Live a Life of Prayer (1 Tim. 2:8).
The more prayer the more spiritual power (Rom. 12:12; Eph. 6:18; Phil. 4:6; Col. 4:2; 1 Thess. 5:17; James 5:16).

3. He Should Live a Life of Faith (Heb. 11:6).
New life began with faith—let it continue (Col. 1:4, 23; 2:5; 2 Thess. 1:3; Heb. 11:32–34).

4. He Should Live a Life of Separation (Heb. 13:12–13).
Separation from the world, the flesh and the devil (Ex. 32:26; Isa. 52:11; John 15:19 with 17:14–16; 2 Cor. 7:1; 1 John 2:15–17).

5. He Should Live a Life of Self-Denial (Gal. 5:24).
Paul left no doubt as to his thought on the subject (Matt. 16:24–25; Rom. 8:13; Eph. 4:22–25; Col. 3:5–10; Titus 2:11–14; 1 Peter 2:11–12).

6. He Should Live a Life of Devotion (1 Chron. 29:5).
Consecration, dedication, sanctification (Rom. 12:1–2; 2 Cor. 9:7; 1 Peter 2:5).

7. He Should Live a Life of Service (Heb. 12:28).
When Jesus takes command He always commissions (Mark 16:15; Luke 5:3–4; 24:47–48; John 12:26).   *C. C. Maple*

THE CHILD OF GOD SHOULD BE STEADFAST

In Faith	(1 Peter 5:9)
In Work	(1 Cor. 15:58)
In Looking	(Acts 1:10)
In Doctrine	(Acts 2:42)
In Mind	(Ruth 1:18)

Pegs for Preachers

SECRET OF VICTORY OVER THE WORLD

1. Keep from it (James 1:27).
The place of separation is the place of power. To "keep unspotted" means not to be stained, therefore we must not be near the world, but keep from the range of its mud-slinging.

2. Take Christ's victory over it.
His Word is, "I have overcome the world," therefore He bids us, "Be of good cheer" (John 16:33). See the three references to Christ and "this world" in John's gospel: 12:31; 14:30; 16:11.

3. Believe you have the victory over it.
"This is the victory that overcometh the world, even our faith" (1 John 5:4–5); and the reasons are, because we have been begotten of God, and because we love Him.

4. Recognize the Lord's indwelling presence.
"Ye have overcome them, because greater is He that is in you than He that is in the world" (1 John 4:4). The Lord within keeps the world without.

5. It is your enemy.
Remember, the world is an enemy, and we are not to have fellowship with it (James 4:4); for if we do, we side with an enemy.

6. Don't love it.
The uncompromising and specific command of the Lord is, "Love not the world" (1 John 2:15).

7. Recognize your place.
Call to mind the prayer of Christ about the world, and remember you are taken "out of it," sent into it, but not of it, and He prays you may be kept from it (John 17:6–7, 14–15).

Selected

THREE EXAMPLES OF DEALING WITH GOD

Waiting on God	(Ps. 130:5)—David
Walking with God	(Gen. 5:22)—Enoch
Working for God	(Heb. 11:7)—Noah

500 Scripture Outlines

STAND FAST IN THE LORD

Philippians 4:1

1. **We Are to Stand Fast in the Faith (1 Cor. 16:13).**
   In many places the faith is in danger (Jude 3, 20–21).

2. **We Are to Stand Fast in Christian Liberty (Gal. 5:1).**
   Were you ever in spiritual bondage (Gal. 2:16; Titus 3:5)?

3. **We Are to Stand Fast in Gospel Teaching (1 Cor. 9:16–17).**
   Many things taught as Gospel that are not Gospel (2 Thess. 2:15; 2 Tim. 4:2; Titus 2:1).

4. **We Are to Stand Fast in Our Christian Fellowship (Phil. 1:27).**
   This is necessary in order to strengthen the church (Acts 2:42, 46–47; Heb. 10:25; 1 John 1:3, 7).

5. **We Are to Stand Fast in Our Progress as Christians (Phil. 4:1).**
   Believers are to "keep moving forward" (Ps. 78:9; 2 Peter 1:3–7).

6. **We Are to Stand Fast in Our Christian Warfare (Eph. 6:13–14).**
   The Christian life is more than a parade (2 Tim. 2:3–4; 4:7–8).

7. **We Are to Stand Fast in Our Victorious Living (1 Thess. 3:8).**
   It was never God's plan that there be defeat (Rom. 12:1–2; Titus 2:11–14). *C. C. Maple*

DOUBLE TITLES GIVEN TO THE LORD JESUS

I. The Author and Finisher of Our Faith—(Heb. 12:2)

II. The Apostle and High Priest of Our Profession—(Heb. 3:1)

III. The Shepherd and Bishop of Our Souls—(1 Peter 2:25)

Twelve Baskets Full

THE STEWARDSHIP OF TIME

2 Peter 3:11

Introduction

Just as certainly as we are responsible for use of our possessions, we are to be careful stewards of our time. In the truest sense we are all living on borrowed time.

I. Recognition

"Seeing then that all these things shall be dissolved."

A. We must realize that all material things are passing.

B. The admonition is to "redeem the time." Buy it up and invest it for eternity.

II. Resolution

A. People should resolve to be the persons they "ought . . . to be."

B. Systematize time. Avoid waste.

III. Reformation

"In all holy conversation and godliness."

A. Personal habits will be improved.

B. The church will prosper through you.

R. C. Kratzer

PICTURE OF A RIGHTEOUS MAN

The Way	of the Righteous—(Ps. 1:6)
The Inheritance	of the Righteous—(Ps. 37:29)
The Gladness	of the Righteous—(Ps. 64:10)
The Flourishing	of the Righteous—(Ps. 92:12)
The Remembrance	of the Righteous—(Ps. 112:6)
The Thanksgiving	of the Righteous—(Ps. 140:13)
The Safety	of the Righteous—(Prov. 18:10)
The Recompense	of the Righteous—(Prov. 11:21)

Pegs for Preachers

WHAT EVERY CHRISTIAN SHOULD DO

1. **Walk More Consistently**
   "Walk circumspectly" (Eph. 5:15).

2. **Work More Heartily**
   "Whatsoever ye do," etc. (Col. 3:23).

3. **Suffer More Patiently**
   "Suffer . . . take it patiently" (1 Peter 2:20).

4. **Fight More Faithfully**
   "Fight the good fight of faith" (1 Tim. 6:12).

5. **Live More Contentedly**
   "Be content . . . as ye have" (Heb. 13:5).

6. **Pray More Constantly**
   "Pray without ceasing" (1 Thess. 5:17).

7. **Preach More Earnestly**
   "Be ye reconciled to God" (2 Cor. 5:20).

8. **Long for Him More Intently**
   "That love His appearing" (2 Tim. 4:8).

Selected

THE LORD'S PEOPLE

Are described in the Word as
   I.   A Chosen People (Deut. 7:6; 2:9)
   II.   A Redeemed People (Exod. 15:13; Eph. 1:7)
   III. A Peculiar People (Deut. 14:2; Titus 2:14)
   IV.   A Separated People (Exod. 33:16; John 15:19)
   V.   A Holy People (Deut. 7:6; 1 Peter 1:15)
   VI.   A Happy People (Deut. 33:29; John 15:11)

500 Bible Subjects

THE GIFT OF ETERNAL LIFE

2 Timothy 1:9–10; John 10:10

Eternal Life Is—

1. **The gift of God (Rom. 6:23).**

2. **A gift of grace (2 Thess. 1:12; Rom. 5:8).**

3. **A twofold gift (John 3:16; 1 Tim. 2:6; Eph. 5:2).**

An Unlimited Gift—

1. **Christ gave Himself a ransom for all (1 Tim. 2:6, 4).**

2. **He is the Savior of all (1 Tim. 4:10).**

3. **In Him all shall be made alive (1 Cor. 15:22).**

4. **He is not willing that any should perish (2 Peter 3:9).**

The Recipients—

1. **Whosoever will (Rev. 22:17).**

2. **Whosoever that believeth (John 3:15–16; 6:47).**

3. **Him that cometh unto Me (John 6:37).**

E. A. Hewitt

MIND NOT EARTHLY THINGS

Set your affection on things above, not on things on the earth (Col. 3:2).

I. **Worldly Things Should Not Engross Us**
   A. Because they are beneath us
   B. Because they are unsuited to us
   C. Because they cannot satisfy us
   D. Because they are unnecessary to us

II. **Heavenly Things Are Worthy of Our Love**
   A. Because they are suitable to our natures
   B. Because our relations are there
   C. Because our treasure is there

Pulpit Germs

THE SPIRIT-FILLED CHRISTIAN

And they were all filled with the Holy Spirit, and began to speak with other tongues, as the Spirit gave them utterance (Acts 2:4).

The whole book of Acts is radiant with the stories of those whose souls were filled with the Spirit, and shows us the glorious effect of the Holy Spirit's indwelling in the lives of the early disciples. Four examples:

1. *Peter*—Ease and boldness in speech; unswerving fidelity to Christ.

2. *Stephen*—Angelic sweetness and patience, courageous testimony, heroic fortitude.

3. *Philip*—Persuasive reasoning and patient persistence in winning individual souls to Christ.

4. *Paul*—Splendid consecration in giving up his high social status and casting in his lot with the despised Nazarenes, and devoting his great talents to the service of Christ.

J. Ellis

WHAT CHRISTIANS POSSESS

They have redemption (Eph. 1:6–7).

They have everlasting life (John 3:36).

They have a great High Priest (Heb. 4:14).

They have the Holy Spirit (1 Cor. 6:19).

They have the promises of God (James 1:12).

They have the sure word of prophecy (2 Peter 1:19).

They have a sure hope (Heb. 6:19–20).

Selected

CHRISTIANS—*What should they be?*

Imitators of God as children (Eph. 5:1).

Strong in the Lord (Eph. 6:10).

Doers of the Word (James 1:22).

Be ye holy (1 Peter 1:16).

Sober and prayerful (1 Peter 6:7).

Faithful unto death (Rev. 2:10).

The Preacher's Tool Basket

THE CHRISTIAN'S SECRET OF ENDURANCE

1 Peter 1:8–9

I. **Loving**
   Without having seen Him (John 20:29).

II. **Believing**
   Without seeing—walking by faith and not by sight.

III. **Rejoicing**
   With unutterable joy.

IV. **Obtaining**
   A. The salvation of one's soul as the outcome of one's faith.
   B. So we hold on and so we hold out.

R. E. Price

TRUTHS ABOUT TRUSTING GOD

Proverbs 16:20

"Godliness is profitable for all things." The most intelligent have given their verdict in favor of godly living—and though some may see it through a false medium, or be so enchanted by the pleasures of sense as for a time to forget it, yet in the hour of solemn and deliberate thought, they agree with Solomon, "Whoever trusts in the LORD, happy is he" (Prov. 12:20, NKJV). The holy fruits of godly living, its substantial pleasures, its powers to preserve from evil, its supporting influence in times of calamity, and its glorious effects on futurity, must endear it to every sober and intelligent mind.

I. The Important Principle to Be Exercised—"Trust."

Trust signifies dependence, reliance, confidence. *Trust* in the Old Testament and *faith* in the New Testament are synonymous (Eph. 1:12–13). It implies—

A. A deep sense of our sinfulness and helplessness, and a knowledge of Christ the Mediator. The man who trusts in God is savingly illuminated on these subjects.

B. A knowledge of God's gracious character as the object of trust. "They that know," etc. (Ps. 9:10).

Safely to trust in any man, we must have an approving knowledge of his character. The infinite love of God; the rich provisions of His grace; the pleasure He takes in the prosperity of His servants, etc., warrant the soul to trust Him. Trust in God is opposed to self-confidence, to trust in the law, moral duties, etc. This would be like a man treading on soft yielding ground, incapable of supporting the feet. The man who trusts in God through Christ places his soul on a Rock firm and immovable (Isa. 28:16; Heb. 13:8).

C. A constant reliance upon God for all temporal and spiritual blessings. For food; for pardon and acceptance; for peace, preservation, and the fulfillment of His promises; the keeping of the soul, and its salvation, against that day. Paul knew whom he believed. He who trusts God, expects and waits for the manifestation of His love.

II. Its Gracious Influence—"Happy is he."

A. He has the favorable *testimony of God* (Heb. 11:5–6).

B. He enjoys the infinite *blessings of salvation*. He is saved.

Delivered from the wrath to come. "Kept by the power of God" (1 Peter 1:5).

C. Trust *ennobles, elevates, and dignifies him*, making him more excellent than his neighbor. It sanctifies.

D. It *cheers and supports him* in the darkest season. It did Abraham (Heb. 11:8–9) and Job, who said, "Though he slay me, yet will I trust in him." And David and Habakkuk (Hab. 3:17–18).

E. By it he *conquers his enemies*. The world (1 John 5:4–5); Satan (Eph. 6:16).

F. It is *productive* of the hope of heaven (Heb. 11:1).

It produces joy. It calms the mind. "Thou wilt keep him in perfect peace whose mind is stayed on thee" (Isa. 26:3). The idea is taken from an army besieged; the place is impregnable; the munitions of war are abundant; the stores of provision are sufficiently ample. The attack against it may be terrible and furious, but the soldiers of the garrison are at peace, calm, collected and confident, knowing where their strength lies.

G. Lastly, it *conquers death* (1 Cor. 15:55–57).

102 Sketches and Skeletons

CHRIST'S RELATION TO THE BELIEVER

Ephesians 2:14–22

1. **Christ Our Peace (vv. 14–15)**

2. **Christ Our Reconciliation (vv. 16–17)**

3. **Christ Our Mediator (vv. 18–19)**

4. **Christ Our Foundation (vv. 20–22)**

Lorraine Shearman

THE PATHWAY OF DISCIPLESHIP

Matthew 11:29; 16:24

If we will be disciples we must learn to observe:

I. Denial of Self

Peter, the mouthpiece of God: "Thou art the Christ, the Son of the Living God" . . . a little later is the mouthpiece of Satan (denials). To deny self does not mean that we should become hermits or ascetics for a year, a few days, or a day and deny "things"; but it means that we deny "self . . . the self-life." How do we deny? Peter said, "I do not know Him." We must say to self, "I do not know you and will not obey you."

II. Pathway of Discipleship

"Take up his cross," not, "Carry your cross with a smile." What did the cross mean to our Lord? "Suffering." It means the same for us! The world is no friend of Christ today. The principles of faith in Christ are the opposite of the principles of the world.

The cross, an instrument of death . . . for the Lord . . . and for us. Our position in Christ: United with Him in His death. We should daily walk as those who are dead unto sin and alive unto God. A dead man is not attracted to the things about him.

III. Pathway of Discipleship

" . . . and follow Me." "Keep on following Me."

A. The Lord Jesus Christ, as a man, was utterly dependent on the Father. How much more, we.

B. Obeying the Father: Complete obedience.

C. Fellowship between the Father and the Son was broken once because of our disobedience and His obedience.

D. "Let this mind be in you." We can only follow Him on a pathway of humility.

Selected

THE CHRIST LIFE

For me to live is Christ, and to die is gain (Phil. 1:21).

1. **A Life of Obedience (Acts 9:6; Heb. 10:9)**

2. **A Life of Service (1 Cor. 9:22)**

3. **A Life of Power (Matt. 28:18; Phil. 4:13)**

4. **A Life of Sacrifice (John 15:13; Phil. 3:7)**

5. **A Life of Separation (2 Cor. 6:14–18; Heb. 7:26)**

6. **A Life of Suffering (2 Cor. 4:10–11)**

7. **A Life of Victory (Phil. 2:9–11; 1 Cor. 15:57; Rom. 8:37)**

Treasures of Bible Truth
William H. Schweinfurth

PAUL'S DESIRE IN PHILIPPIANS

To KNOW Christ (3:10)

To WIN Christ (3:8)

To Be CONFORMED to Christ (3:10)

To MAGNIFY Christ (1:20)

To Be FOUND in Christ (3:9)

To REJOICE in Christ (2:16)

To Be WITH Christ (1:23)

Pegs for Preachers

THE RESOURCES OF THE CHRISTIAN

For in him dwelleth all the fullness of the Godhead bodily (Col. 2:9).

1. **The Lord Jesus Christ Is Our Passover**
   (1 Cor. 5:7)

2. **The Lord Jesus Christ Is Our Salvation**
   (Luke 2:27–30; 19:9; Isa. 12:2; 49:6)

3. **The Lord Jesus Christ Is Our Life**
   (Col. 3:4; 1 John 5:12)

4. **The Lord Jesus Christ Is Our Peace**
   (Eph. 2:13–14; Col. 1:20)

5. **The Lord Jesus Christ Is Our Wisdom, and Righteousness, and Sanctification, and Redemption**
   (1 Cor. 1:30)

6. **The Lord Jesus Christ Is Our Strength**
   (Phil. 3:13; Eph. 6:10; Ps. 18:2)

7. **The Lord Jesus Christ Is Our Victory**
   (1 Cor. 15:57; Rom. 8:37)

Treasures of Bible Truth

THREE POSITIONS OF THE BELIEVER

Philippians 3

1. **Found in Christ (v. 9)—His Place.**

2. **Fellowship with Christ (v. 10)—His Privilege.**

3. **Fashioned like Christ (v. 21)—His Prospect.**

Five Hundred Children's Subjects
John Ritchie

HOW TO KNOW CHRIST BETTER

That I may know him (Phil. 3:10).

To come to know Christ better was the first consuming desire of the heart of Paul after he met Him on the way to Damascus. We come to know Christ, first of all, by the new birth. Paul had passed this experience of grace. He applied himself definitely to know Christ better. All should long to know Him intimately. We make the following suggestions to help you to attain this end:

1. Spend Much Time in Meditation.

After Paul met Christ his first move was to go alone with God for a long season of meditation on the meaning of the experience. During these months of meditation he received the Gospel "by the revelation of Jesus Christ" (Gal. 1:12).

The Lord gave Paul the clearest and most perfect understanding of the Gospel any man has had. We can come to know Christ better by quiet meditation.

2. Study Constantly the Lord's Message.

If we are to come to know Christ intimately, we must make the most of the Bible. The entire message of the Bible centers about Christ. We must know the Bible if we would know Christ well.

3. Speak Often with the Lord.

We come to know people by talking with them and hearing them speak. So with the Lord Jesus we come to know Him by talking with Him. In prayer we speak to the Father and hear Him speak to us.

4. Seek Fellowship with Other Christians.

Even though Paul did not go immediately to Jerusalem to see the apostles, he eventually did go, and had days of fellowship with Peter and James. Fellowship with consecrated and well-informed Christians may mean much to young Christians in coming to know Christ and His will and way for life.

5. Serve the Savior in Sincerity.

Jesus said, "Take my yoke upon you, and learn of me." In other words, when a Christian gets under the problems of the Savior and serves with Him, he will come to know Him.

We will know Him when we think with Him. We will know

Him when we suffer with Him. We will see His love for the lost and desire to have the same when we serve with Him. Paul served with Christ in a matchless way.

Set your heart to know Christ better and better. In meditation, Bible study, prayer, fellowship and service, seek to know Him and the fellowship of His suffering and the power of His resurrection.

Selected

THE SCOPE OF CHRISTIAN EXPERIENCE

For we are his workmanship, created in Christ
Jesus unto good works . . . (Eph. 2:10).

The soul's sublime experience is salvation by grace through faith in the Lord Jesus Christ. The fullness of this gracious experience has a wide scope.

1. This Experience Has the Upward Reach

"We are his workmanship." We become new creatures in Christ by the grace of God. It is the work of God the Father. The experience is with the Father, the Lord Jesus Christ and the Holy Spirit. Faith must reach upward and take hold of the grace of God by faith.

2. This Experience Has the Inward Reach

"Created in Christ Jesus." In conviction the soul realizes it is in sin. In repentance it turns away from sin and by faith unto Christ. In regeneration the soul is made new in Christ and becomes a new creation with new hopes, new desires, new thoughts, new purposes, and new determinations.

3. This Experience Has the Outward Reach

"Unto good works." God has a purpose in salvation. The saved soul will reach out to others for Christ. It will desire to become a laborer with God for a lost world.

Sermons in Outline, Jerome O. Williams

CHRISTIAN CHARACTER

Be ye kind one to another, tenderhearted, forgiving one another,
even as God for Christ's sake hath forgiven you (Eph. 4:32).

This text gives the extent, the experience, the expression, and the best example of Christian character.

1. The Extent of Christian Character.

"Be ye kind." When a person is born again by the Spirit of God, he becomes a new creature in Christ. The inherent nature of this life will then become gentle, gracious, kind, good and benevolent. Such characteristics will dominate the entire life. These characteristics make up the real Christian personality.

2. The Experience in Christian Character.

"Be ye . . . tenderhearted." In its relations to others, the Christian character is easily moved to love, to pity, to sorrow, to sympathy. Such life will be able to place itself in the position of others and feel as they feel.

It will move with compassion for others as Jesus was moved.
It will quickly lend a helping hand to the person in need.
It will spend itself for others.

3. The Expression of Christian Character.

"Forgiving one another." Christian character will readily express itself toward others in being willing to forgive those who sin against it.

A forgiving spirit is Christlike, for on the cross Christ prayed for those who crucified Him, saying, "Father, forgive them; for they know not what they do."

Jesus taught that His followers should be willing to forgive a limitless number of times. Christian character expresses itself in willingness to forgive.

4. The Example of Christian Character.

"Even as God for Christ's sake hath forgiven you." The example of God the Father is here held up as the ideal for the Christian. This is the most sublime ideal. This is the highest example of Christian character. It is the highest and holiest ideal and should be before every Christian.

Author Unknown

PROGRESS IN GRACE

I.   Saved by Grace (Eph. 2:8).

A. We need to acquaint ourselves with the grace of God: that wonderful new thing that Christ revealed to men.

1. He showed it long ago in His life, teaching, and death for sinners, but many still do not know anything about it: know no other way of holiness but by works of law.

B. We need to verify in our own experience that a saving virtue resides in the grace of God.

1. Let us try to realize what it means that the God we had offended by our sin, whom we had ignored by our indifference, has ever been looking on us in love and planning to make us fit to enjoy Himself forever. Has the grace of God saved you from sin?

II.   Standing in Grace: established in it (Rom. 5:2).

III.   Taught by Grace (Titus 2:12).

A. We cannot possibly be affected by the grace of God without its having a revolutionary effect on our conduct.

IV.   Growing in Grace (2 Peter 3:18).

A. As the years go on we shall get larger and fuller views of God's grace.

V.   Speaking in Grace (Col. 4:6).

A. We shall not be able to keep the blessing to ourselves; we shall speak of the grace of God and in the grace of God.

B. Our way of speaking to others should give them some idea of how Christ spoke to men.

C. Our conversation is to be always with grace, tempered with salt which saves from corruption.

VI.   Ministering Grace (Eph. 4:29).

A. Our relationship with others should be of such a character that it helps to form them also in the likeness of Christ.   .

B. All our conduct toward others should tend to show them more and more of the beauty of the grace as revealed in Christ.

VII.   Who Is Sufficient for These Things?

We can neither receive nor show the grace of God in our own strength, but only through Christ's enabling, in answer to prayer.

100 Sermon Outlines

THE FRUIT OF THE SPIRIT

But the fruit of the Spirit is love, joy, peace, longsuffering, gentleness, goodness, faith, meekness, temperance (Gal. 5:22–23).

We have "the works of the flesh," but we do not read of "the fruits of the Spirit," but in the singular number—fruit.

The nine graces are one fruit.

I. **All the Other Fruits of the Spirit Are Only the Expansion of the First.**

    A. Joy is love triumphing.

    B. Peace is love resting.

    C. Long-suffering is love under the great trials.

    D. Gentleness is love under the little trials of life.

    E. Goodness is love going forth into action.

    F. Faith is love sitting and receiving back again to its own bosom.

    G. Meekness is love controlling the passions of the mind.

    H. Temperance, the same love subduing the passions of the body.

The law of the Spirit is all contained in one word, and the unity of the whole Christian character is "love." Fruit is not fruit if it is not sweet. What is anything to God until there is love in it? Therefore love stands first.

II. **There Is a Law of Growth about the Spirit of God in a Man.**

    A. This is as sure as the law which regulates the growth and development of any plant.

        1. This truth is wrapped up in the metaphor "the fruit of the Spirit."

        2. If there is not advance in the image of Christ, it is because the work of the Holy Spirit is obstructed, for the Spirit, in Himself, always essentially grows.

III. **To Be Fruit-Bearers We Must Be Engrafted into the True Vine.**

    A. If there is one state more solemn than another it is the leafy state.

        1. What if Jesus, drawing nigh to any one of us and finding nothing but leaves, should punish the barrenness which is willful by the barrenness which is judicial: "No man eat fruit of thee hereafter forever"?

Three Hundred Outlines on the New Testament

HOW TO BECOME A CHRISTIAN:
An Evangelistic Message

Acts 2:37–38

Introduction

These inquirers were sinners and wanted to become Christians. They asked how they might become Christians, and Peter answered their question.

I. One Must Believe That God Is (Heb. 11:6)
A. That is, believe there is a God.
B. Believe that He will reward a sinner, forgive him.
C. One must believe the Bible is God's Word.
D. These inquiring Jews believed in God and the Bible.

II. One Must Be Convicted of His Sins
A. The Holy Spirit convicts of sin (John 16:7–8).
B. God draws men toward Christ (John 6:44).
C. The inquiring Jews were deeply convicted.
D. The Gospel had reached their hearts.
E. God had spoken to them by the Gospel and Spirit.

III. Repentance Is the Next Step
A. Except you repent you shall perish (Luke 13:3).
B. Repentance is a command of God (Acts 17:30).
C. John demanded it of his converts (Matt. 3:5–8).
D. Christ preached on the subject of repentance (Mark 1:15).

IV. Accept Christ by Faith
A. Must by faith accept the free gift.
B. If a friend offered you a gift you would not receive it unless you accepted it.
C. Christ offers pardon after you have met conditions, but you must accept to receive.

V. God's Part in Our Redemption
A. To provide the atonement. He did in Christ.
B. To convict or draw the sinner. This He is doing.
C. When you fully decide, confessing your sins in faith, He will forgive (1 John 1:9).

Conclusion

Why be lost? God will do all of His part and help you to do yours.

John C. Jernigan

WHAT CHRIST HAS DONE FOR US

1. **Died for us (1 Cor. 15:3)**
2. **Bore our sins (1 Peter 2:24)**
3. **Loved us (Rev. 1:5)**
4. **Saved us (Titus 3:5)**
5. **Washed us (Rev. 1:5)**
6. **Quickened us (Eph. 2:5)**
7. **Translated us (Col. 1:13)**
8. **Made us Kings (Rev. 1:6)**
9. **Called us (2 Tim. 1:9)**
10. **Delivered us (2 Cor. 1:10)**
11. **Has begotten us (1 Peter 1:3)**
12. **Raised us (Eph. 2:6)**
13. **Has given us the victory (1 Cor. 15:57)**
14. **Blessed us (Eph. 1:3)**

Twelve Baskets Full

WHY CHRIST WENT BACK TO HEAVEN

Acts 1:9

1. To prepare a place for us (John 14:2; 1 Cor. 2:9; 2 Cor. 5:1).

2. To be our High Priest (Heb. 2:17; 4:14–15; 7:25).

3. To satisfy God's righteousness (Ps. 110:1; Heb. 9:15–25).

4. To send His Holy Spirit (John 16:7; Acts 1:8).

5. To intercede for us with the Father (1 Tim. 2:5; 1 John 2:1).

6. To be honored by His Father (Phil. 2:6–11).

A. B. Carrero

THE TENDERNESS OF GOD

As a father pities (Ps. 103:13).

As a mother comforts (Isa. 66:13).

As a hen gathers (Matt. 23:37).

As an eagle flutters (Deut. 32:11).

As a nurse cherishes (1 Thess. 2:7).

As a shepherd seeks (Ezek. 34:12).

As a refiner sits (Mal. 3:3).

As a bridegroom rejoices (Isa. 62:5).

D. L. Moody

THE MARKS OF A CHRISTIAN

1 John 1–2

A CHRISTIAN . . .

Walks in the Light of God's Word:

"If we say that we have fellowship with him, and walk in darkness, we lie, and do not live by the truth. But if we walk in the light, as he is in the light, we have fellowship one with another, and the blood of Jesus his Son cleanseth us from all sin" (1 John 1:6–7).

A CHRISTIAN . . .

Has Christ as His Example:

"He that saith he abideth in him ought himself also so to walk, even as he walked" (1 John 2:6).

A CHRISTIAN . . .

Has No Love or Place in His Life for the World:

"Love not the world, neither the things that are in the world. If any man love the world, the love of the Father is not in him. For all that is in the world, the lust of the flesh, and the lust of the eyes, and the pride of life, is not of the Father, but is of the world. And the world passeth away, and the lust thereof: but he that doeth the will of God abideth forever" (1 John 2:15–17).

A CHRISTIAN . . .

Is Taught by God's Spirit:

"But the anointing that ye have received of Him abideth in you, and ye need not that any man teach you: but as the same anointing teacheth you of all things, and is truth, and is no lie, and even as it hath taught you, ye shall abide in him" (1 John 2:27).

Selected

SALVATION

(Titus 2:11)

I. Effected Through Grace (2 Tim. 1:9)
II. Merited Through Christ (Rom. 4:25)
III. Revealed Through Mercy (Eph. 2:4–5)
IV. Accepted Through Faith (Heb. 11:6)

THE SIN OF BEING TOO BUSY

1 Kings 20:40

Everyone thinks at times that he is the busiest person in town. Entering the office, store, or mill, one hears the statement, "This is my busy day." Approach the ordinary individual concerning some project aside from the regular routine, and he will likely say, "I haven't time."

Because folks are busy with big business is no reason why they should neglect the claims of the biggest Man in the world. Jesus Christ was both big and busy—none were bigger nor busier. Yet He always found time to be about His Father's business.

Our text springs from the story of battles. The Israelites had beaten the Syrians. The captured leader was marked for punishment and entrusted to a man who, upon a flimsy pretext let the captive escape. His excuse was that he had been too busy for his chief duty.

I. This Is the Notable Sin of Many

We are always busy—too busy to accept Christ or lead others to Him. Jesus warned against the high crime of preoccupation. In the parable of the soils, He lamented the highest life being choked out by the pursuit of other things.

Clutching at the throat of spiritual life are three death-dealing hands.

A. One of them is worldly cares. This means, of course, unnecessary anxiety. It is unrelaxing attention to material things to the exclusion of preparation for the eternal. Subtle in their lure and promising joy, they become devious deceivers.

B. There is deceitfulness of riches. Christ was speaking of the fruitage of worldly toil. The glitter of gold may be as deceptive to one receiving 15 thousand dollars annually as it is to him who receives 150 thousand dollars. Christ warned the prosperous farmer that he could not feed his soul on corn. Unless he controls both production and use of every income, it chokes out eternal life.

C. Then Jesus rebuked the excessive pursuit of things. This may be nothing criminal—just things displacing Him. It may be only tasks, social engagements, business committees—one after another until preoccupation leaves no room for Him. Only the dregs of time, talents, or money are left for the world's Savior.

II. The Sin of Being Too Busy Often Leads to Dodging Duty

Humanity crowds the courtroom when God holds court with sinners. Though not rebellious against God, we may simply kick duty under the bed while we imagine God is not looking our way. Setting profit or pleasure above the welfare of our fellows is sinful. We love God and serve Him only as we love and serve our neighbors. "He that loveth not his brother whom he hath seen, how can he love God whom he hath not seen?"

III. Christ Needs Busy People

Christ needs big men—busy men of big business. His is the biggest business in the world. It is winning men to Christ instead of letting them go to hell because we are too busy. When Lord Kitchener was once approached by a subordinate officer with a recital of reasons for not obeying an order, he replied, "Your reasons for not doing it are the best I ever heard; now go and do it." Our Christ speaks likewise to us.

May we preserve our moral equilibrium, speed up our spiritual development, and live happier lives because we find time for Christ.

Irwin Farmer

THE SEEKING SAVIOR

Hebrews 7:25

I. His Ability to Save
"Able also to save" (Heb. 7:25).
A. Because He died. "Christ died for us" (Rom. 5:8).
B. Because He lives. "He ever liveth" (Heb. 7:25).
C. Because He loves. "Who loved me" (Gal. 2:20).

II. The Extent to Which He Saves
"To the uttermost" (Heb. 7:25).
He saves from:
A. The sin which mastered us (Rom. 6:14).
B. The bondage which enthralled us (Heb. 2:14–15).
C. The wrath which awaited us (1 Thess. 1:10).

III. Those Whom He Saves
"All that come" (Heb. 7:25).
A. Who are to come? Those at a distance (Isa. 57:19).
B. How am I to come? "Just as I am."
C. When am I to come? "Now" (Isa. 1:18).

Author Unknown

TWENTY TRUTHS ABOUT MY
SINS WHEN I TRUST IN JESUS

1. Blotted out (Isa. 43:25; 44:22; Acts 3:19).
2. Borne by another (1 Peter 2:24).
3. Cast behind God's back (Isa. 38:17).
4. Covered (Rom. 4:7).
5. Cast into the depths of the sea (Mic. 7:19).
6. Finished (Dan. 9:24).
7. Forgiven (Col. 2:13).
8. Not beheld (Num. 23:21).
9. Not imputed (Rom. 4:8).
10. Not remembered (Heb. 8:12).
11. Pardoned (Mic. 7:18).
12. Passed away (Zech. 3:4).
13. Purged (Heb. 1:3).
14. Put away (Heb. 7:27).
15. Remitted (Acts 10:43).
16. Removed (Ps. 103:12).
17. Subdued (Mic. 7:19).
18. Sought for and not found (Jer. 50:20).
19. Washed away with blood (1 John 1:7).
20. Taken away (Isa. 7:7).

Selected

THE SUBTLETY OF SECRET SINS

Cleanse me from secret faults (Ps. 19:12).

When the psalmist prays to be cleansed from "secret faults," I understand him to ask to be delivered from the dominion of all secret sins. Secret sins are peculiarly dangerous. They probably harden more hearts, sear more consciences and ruin more souls than do open, daylight sins.

I. Why Are Secret Sins So Dangerous?

A. Change of place and circumstances does not aid you to break away from them.

B. Secret sins produce a continual warfare between the conscience and the desires of the heart.

C. Secret sins return often.

D. Secret sins counteract and destroy the means of grace.

E. Secret sins give the tempter great power over one.

II. What Are Remedies for Secret Sins?

A. Realize they are sins.

B. If you would be cleansed from secret sins, you must be much in prayer.

C. If you would be cleansed from secret sins, avoid temptations.

D. If you would be free from secret sins, be constantly mindful of the presence of God.

Are you not ashamed to commit open sins because men will see you? And should you not be ashamed to commit secret sins, when God sees you?

John Todd

A DIVINE INVITATION

Come unto Me, all you who labor and are heavy laden,
and I will give you rest (Matt. 11:28).

Here is a message for the busy folks of today: The businessman
who comes home after a great business deal, yet knowing just how
little the deal counts in the ultimate things of life; the society woman
who gets inches of newspaper space with descriptions of her parties
and gowns, and yet who has her moments of insight which show
the worthlessness; young men and women, dizzy with the activities
of a busy age, yet who have fears for the safety of the future in their
moments of thoughtfulness—

It is to such as these, and to men and women of every class and
type, that the message of my text comes; it can be universally applied and can be heard as a response to every aching longing.

1. The Preacher's Message Starts with Jesus Christ

Christianity has one thing which no pagan religion can offer. That is Jesus Christ. And He is different from any other person
in the world. This text is meaningful simply because He gave it. To
deepen the Christ consciousness in the world is to deepen God consciousness. Behind all the theologies the thing that Christ has to
offer is simply Jesus Christ. He it is who promises to bring rest to
the weary.

2. To Accept This Invitation Means a Willingness to Take a Definite Step

We do not know just where that step may lead. It means
accepting Jesus and following Him wherever His mind and thoughts
may lead us. The "coming" is the first stage in the process of learning in which willingness to accept is called "taking the yoke." It
seems like a tremendous demand. But upon second look it is similar
to every other demand in life. The college student makes a yielding
to the mind of his instructors when he enters as a freshman. If he
did not agree to sit at the feet of his instructors, his learning would
cease. So with those who follow the Christ.

3. Christ Will Bring Peace of Heart and Mind to Those Who Accept This Invitation

It does not mean that there will not be distress and sorrow,
disturbance and misfortune. But He promises—and thousands have

found that promise true—that in the distresses and anxieties of the world, even in pestilence and affliction, there will be peace of mind.

H. R. L. Sheppard

TEN WAYS TO FOLLOW CHRIST

There are distinct instances where Christ gives the command "Follow Me" and in these instances we have a call of Christ:

1. The call of *salvation* (John 1:43–50).

2. Follow the Lamb as *firstfruits* (Rev. 14:4b).

3. The call of *ownership* (John 10:27).

4. The call to *concentration* (John 21:18–22).

5. The call to *separation* (Matt. 8:22).

6. The call to *self-denial* (Matt. 16:24—deny self, and Mark 10:21—obey).

7. The call to *consecration* (Matt. 19:21).

8. The call to *imitation* (John 12:26).

9. The call of the *compassionate heart* (Matt. 4:19).

10. The call to *Himself* (Matt. 9:9).

Author Unknown

SEVEN TELLTALE MARKS OF A CHRISTIAN

1. A clean heart (Ps. 51:10; Matt. 5:8).
2. A clean association (Ps. 119:53, 63; 2 Cor. 6:14).
3. A clean conversation (Eph. 4:29; 1 Peter 1:15).
4. A clean mind (Eph. 4:22–23; 1 Tim. 4:12).
5. A clean body (2 Cor. 7:1; Heb. 10:22).
6. A clean path (Ps. 97:11; Isa. 42:16; Dan. 12:10).
7. A clean conscience (2 Cor. 1:12; 1 Tim. 3:9).
    Are these marks found in your life?

A. B. Carrero

THE PRECIOUS BLOOD OF CHRIST

1 Peter 1:19

Why Precious?

1. Because it redeems us (1 Peter 1:18–19).
2. Because it brings us near (Eph. 2:13).
3. Because it blots out our sins (Rev. 1:5).
4. Because it brings peace (Col. 1:20).
5. Because it justifies (Rom. 5:9).
6. Because it cleanses from all sin (1 John 1:7).
7. Because it gives boldness in the day of judgment.

Christ left nothing behind on earth but His blood.

D. L. Moody

THE POWER OF CHRIST FOR EVERY NEED

Matthew 8:1–34

Introduction

The greatest sermon ever preached on earth was finished. Jesus left the comparative seclusion of an open-air classroom on the mountain to come down once more into the valley of human need. What happened immediately after the Sermon on the Mount is a marvelous revelation of the power of Christ as the Master to meet every need.

I. Master of Physical Needs (vv. 1–18)

A. Biological disease (vv. 2–3). Leprosy at once gathers together all the symptoms in many physical ailments: aches, bleeding, sharp pain, fever, weakness, anxiety, etc.

B. Nervous disorder (vv. 5–7).

C. Infectious disease (vv. 14–15).

II. Master in Religious Experience (vv. 19–22)

A. Partial understanding of Christ's doctrine (v. 19), "a certain scribe."

B. Other things came ahead of loyalty to Christ (v. 21), "another disciple."

III. Master in Life's Circumstances (vv. 23–34)

A. Storms of life (vv. 23–27).

B. Mental pressure (v. 28).

Les Parrott

LIFE IN CHRIST

(Colossians 3:1–4)

I.   A Resurrected Life (verse 1a).
II. An Elevating Life (verse 1b, 2).
III. A New Life (verse 3a).
IV. A Protected Life (verse 3b).
V.   The Christ Life (verse 4a).
VI. A Hopeful Life (verse 4b).
VII. A Future Life (verse 4c).

Harlen H. Clayton

THE WAY TO PEACE WITH GOD

1 Thessalonians 5

1. Abide in His love—rejoice evermore (5:16).
2. Abide in prayer—He will hear (5:17).
3. Be always thankful—this is God's will (5:18).
4. Be filled with the Spirit—live as a true child of God (5:19).
5. Continue in the study of the Word—your faith will be stronger (5:20; cf. 2 Tim. 3:15).
6. Hold fast that which is good—be faithful (5:21).
7. Stand fast in the liberty of Christ—abstain from sin (5:22).
8. Peace will be the result—the great peace of God (cf. Job 17:9; Rom. 5:1; Gal. 6:9; Phil. 4:7).

A. B. Carrero

THE GREATEST GIFT

John 3:16

God	The Greatest Lover
So Loved	The Greatest Degree
The World	The Greatest Company
That He Gave	The Greatest Act
His Only Begotten Son	The Greatest Gift
That Whosoever	The Greatest Opportunity
Believeth	The Greatest Simplicity
In Him	The Greatest Attraction
Should Not Perish	The Greatest Promise
But	The Greatest Difference
Have	The Greatest Certainty
Everlasting Life	The Greatest Possession

Selected

CONTRASTS BETWEEN SINNERS AND SAINTS

1. SINNERS: **Servants of sin (Rom. 6:16–23).**
   CHRISTIANS: Servants of God (1 Peter 2:15–16).

2. SINNERS: **In bondage (Gal. 5:1).**
   CHRISTIANS: Free (Rom. 6:22).

3. SINNERS: **Children of the Devil (John 8:44).**
   CHRISTIANS: Children of God (Gal. 4:3–7).

4. SINNERS: **A prodigal away from home (Luke 15:13–14).**
   CHRISTIANS: A child at home (Luke 15:20–24).

5. SINNERS: **Sold under sin (Rom. 7:14).**
   CHRISTIANS: Bought with a price (1 Cor. 6:20).

6. SINNERS: **Led captive by the Devil (2 Tim. 2:26).**
   CHRISTIANS: Led by the Spirit (Rom. 8:14).

7. SINNERS: **The wicked flee (Prov. 28:1).**
   CHRISTIANS: Bold as a lion (Prov. 28:1).

8. SINNERS: **Wicked shall perish (Luke 13:3).**
   CHRISTIANS: Righteous shall never perish (John 10:28).

9. SINNERS: **Jesus does not know them (Matt. 25:12).**
   CHRISTIANS: Jesus knows His own (John 10:27).

10. SINNERS: **"Depart" (Matt. 25:41, 46).**
    CHRISTIANS: "Come" (Matt. 25:31, 34).

Author Unknown

A NEW CREATION

2 Corinthians 5:17

Paul triumphantly declares, "If any man be in Christ, he is a new creature; old things are passed away; behold all things are become new." What does this mean?

1. If Any Man Be in Christ He Has a New God

Such is the nature of the human soul that it must have a god, an object of supreme affection. The character of the soul is determined by the character of its god.

2. He Has a New Object of Pursuit

It is a fundamental principle of human action that every man will seek to please his own god. The man who is in Christ, having changed his god, changes, of course, his object of pursuit. Before, his object was to exalt and gratify himself. Now, his object is to please and glorify Jehovah.

3. He Adopts a New Rule of Action

His own will was the rule of action before; now, the revealed will of God. And when his own will comes into competition with the will of God, his language is, "Not my will, but thine be done." This is the habitual desire of his heart. And he exhibits it, not in words only, but in actions.

4. He Lives a New Life—A Life of Faith in the Son of God

This faith is that confidence in Christ which leads the man to feel that what God has said is true, and to treat it as true. Hence, he seeks by prayer and supplication to know what duty is; he listens to the voice of God in revelation, and he has respect to all His commandments.

5. The Man Who Is in Christ Has New Joys

His joys are much more pure, expansive and exalted as are his views, affections and efforts.

6. He Has New Hopes

Now he has a good hope. It arises from having the love of God shed abroad in his heart by the Holy Spirit.

Justin Edwards

LIFE'S GREAT QUESTION ANSWERED

"Sirs," the jailer asked, "what must I do to be saved?" (Acts 16:30–31).

Are there some who need the answer to the greatest question of life? To such there is no other answer to give than that given by the apostle Paul in the text.

I. What Precedes the Act of Faith in the Experience of the Sinner?

There was, previous to the jailer's faith and essential to it, a conviction first of his guilt, secondly of his danger, and therefore, of his need of salvation, and of a Savior. If one is truly convinced that he is a sinner, justly condemned for his sins, lost unless he obtains mercy through Christ, he needs wait for nothing more. Why should he wait?

II. Let Us Look at the Object of Faith

"Believe," says Paul, "in the Lord Jesus Christ." Christ, and Christ alone, is the object of faith.

III. Let Us Consider the Act of Faith

Faith in Christ is simply confidence or trust in Him. It involves assent to the truth as it is in Jesus, but it is much more than this; it is the confidence of the heart in Him, and the approval of the way of salvation by Him. "With the heart man believeth . . ."

IV. Let Us Look at the Results of Faith

A. On the side of God is His justification of the sinner.
B. There is His acceptance of believers.
C. There is His bestowment of His Spirit on the believer.
D. On the part of the believer there is peace and joy.
E. Another result of faith is obedience.
F. The final result of faith is eternal life. The great issues of faith are in eternity. Who can show us the everlasting difference between a lost soul and a saved soul?

  1. The terms of salvation are easy and simple.
  2. The time for the exercise of this faith is now.
  3. The results of faith are most urgent motives to its immediate exercise.

W. W. Woodworth

WHAT DOES IT MEAN TO BE LOST?

Luke 19:10

The child of God may be lost from fellowship with God and needs to be found; but it is a different thing for a soul to be lost in the sense that it needs to be saved. In Luke 15:4 we are told that Christ goes out after the sheep until He finds it; but this must not be confused with the words of our text, "For the Son of man is come to seek and to save that which was lost."

1. Every Individual Born into This World Inherits the Fallen Nature of Adam

This is called the doctrine of total depravity. This doctrine is not understood by many. It means that people are depraved in that they can do nothing which is acceptable unto God.

This condition described by the words, "dead in trespasses and sins," is that the spirit and soul of man are separated from God and are helpless to return to God. The Bible is emphatic when stating the truth that the unsaved, left to their own volition, will not turn to God.

The individual may not be depraved because of his own sin any more than he is responsible for his own ignorance in being born in the world. But he must be saved.

2. Men Are Deathbound Because of Sin

Here again the individual is not responsible. The Bible gives just one reason for this "deathbound." It is because of the sin of Adam.

It must be discerned that the judgment of death which fell upon Adam and his posterity is not physical death alone; it includes both spiritual death and the "second" death.

3. Judgment Rests Now upon Men

This is because God has made a decree which reaches to all men of this age. This decree declares that all unsaved people are "under sin."

It is not difficult to see that to be under sin is a specific judgment from God which is peculiar to the present age; for in no other age has it ever been true that "there is no difference between Jew and Gentile."

All men are under sin until they are saved by grace. God is now calling both Jew and Gentile. Both must go through the same saving process.

4. Men Are Lost Because of Sins They Have Committed

The Scriptures declare that all have sinned and that there is none righteous. The first sin of Adam was an indifference to the demands of God. We commit sins in the same careless way. There is a vast difference between God's conception of sin and man's. But God has the twofold cure. He freely forgives and He freely justifies.

5. Men Are Lost Because They Are in the Power of Satan

Not only is salvation of such a supernatural character that no human being could ever hope to accomplish it for himself, but all that enters in his lost condition can be remedied by God alone, and even God can undertake the salvation of a soul only as He is rendered free to do so through the death of Christ for that soul.

L. S. Chafer

THE STRAIT GATE

Strive to enter in at the strait gate; for many, I say unto you, will seek to enter in, but shall not be able (Luke 13:24).

I. The Gate Which Is Most Desirable to Enter.

A. Because it is the gate of the City of Refuge.
B. Because it is the gate of a home.
C. Because it leads to a blessed feast.
D. Because the loss of those outside the gate is too terrible.

II. There Is a Crowd of People Who Will Seek to Enter and Will Not Be Able.

There is a difference between seeking and striving.

A. Some are unable to enter in because the pride of life will not let them.

B. Some are unable to enter because they seek to take sin with them.

C. Some are unable to enter because they want to postpone the matter until tomorrow.

D. Some think they are in and have mistaken the outside for the inside.

Three Hundred Outlines on the New Testament

TRANSFORMED BY GRACE

Psalm 40:1–3

Within the compass of these three brief verses such great subjects as sin, salvation, security, song and service are treated.

1. Sin

Sin heads the list. Under the figure of a horrible pit filled with miry clay, into which the unwary traveler sinks to his death, the subtle workings of sin and Satan are seen. Sin is a treacherous swamp. Its dangers are not apparent to the light-hearted men and women who argue that they can do certain things that they know to be wrong without being harmed by them. There are hundreds of people who are now held in the bonds of sin who would have been repelled by the picture of themselves a dozen years before. I can think of nothing worse than a place where eternal sin exists. Hell is such a place.

2. Salvation

Salvation is sin's antidote. Or to carry on the figure, it is deliverance from a horrible pit.

"This poor Chinaman was in a deep well. I cried for Confucius to help me. He came and looked at me and said, 'Poor Chinaman, it is too bad that you are down so far. If you could only get out, I could help you, and I could keep you from getting in again.' But I could not get out. He could not reach me, and so he had no help for me. Then I cried for Buddha. He came and wept over me and said, 'I am sure that I could help you if you could only get out.' He, too, was unable to reach me. Finally I heard some missionaries talking about one Jesus who comes right down where men are and lifts them out of the horrible pit. I cried to Him, and He came to the place where I was and lifted me" (a Chinese interpretation of salvation).

3. Security

"He set my feet upon a rock, and established my goings."

People hesitate to yield to Christ because they fear that they will make a shipwreck of their faith. They dread a falling away and a return to sin. They fail to realize that the *keeping* power of Christ is as great as His *saving* power.

4. **Song**

"He hath put a new song in my mouth."
Birds with gladder songs o'erflow,
Flowers with deeper beauty shine,
Since I know, as now I know,
I am his and he is mine."

5. **Service**

"Many shall see it, and fear, and trust."
When a poor, hopeless, worthless sinner is established on the Rock of Ages, he ceases to be a liability and becomes an asset to society. He is saved to serve.

P. W. Philpott

A GLORIOUS EXPERIENCE

Galatians 2:20

1. We are crucified with Christ (Rom. 6:6, 11).

2. Buried with Him in baptism (Rom. 6:4; Col. 2:12).

3. Raised with Him (Rom. 6:4–6; Eph. 2:6).

4. Joint-heirs with Him (Matt. 25:23; Rom. 8:17).

5. Sit together with Him in heavenly places (Eph. 2:6).

6. Looking like Him (Phil. 3:21; 1 John 3:2).

7. Forever with Him (John 14:1–3; 1 Thess. 4:17).

A. B. Carrero

THE PRICE THAT WAS PAID

1 Corinthians 6:20

Introduction

We were condemned to death at the time Christ paid for our redemption; thus we have no rightful claim on ourselves.

I. Why Was a Ransom Necessary?
A. We were under a death sentence.
B. We were condemned to destruction.
C. We were hopeless.

II. What We Were Not Redeemed With
A. Not redeemed of ourselves.
B. No other man had the price.
C. Not redeemed with silver or gold (1 Peter 1:18).
D. Silver and gold buys everything else.
E. Heaven with its walls of jasper, streets of gold, gates of pearl, would not pay the price.
F. The angels did not have the price.

III. What Was the Price and How Paid?
A. Jesus was the price.
B. God gave Him as a manifestation of His divine love for the world (John 3:16).
C. Christ left all and came in poverty to redeem the world.
D. His love was manifested in His untiring ministry.

IV. It Took All He Had to Pay the Price
A. His leaving home would not pay it.
B. His preaching would not pay it.
C. His prayers would not pay it.
D. Persecutions, such as stoning, scourging, false accusations, spitting in His face and smiting Him did not pay it.
E. It took death in the most cruel form.
F. He would have liked to pay it without death.
G. His prayers were to, "Let this cup pass."
H. When He took it He became willing and gave all.

Conclusion

He gave all for the redemption of the world and yet many are dying without the benefit. For those who reject Him, His sacrifice was in vain.

John C. Jernigan

HE GAVE HIMSELF

Galatians 1:4

Through the Bible from Genesis 1:29 to Revelation 21:6, God says, "I have given," or "I give," or "I will give."

I. He Gave Himself for Whom?

A. For many (Matt. 20:28).

B. For all. This certainly means all mankind. Note the following reference: 1 Timothy 2:6, "Who gave Himself a ransom for *all*" (see also 2 Cor. 5:14–15 and Heb. 2:9).

C. For the world (see John 1:29; 3:16–17; 1 John 2:2). This, of course, means the world of mankind, human beings. There is no possible way of twisting this to make it mean merely a fraction of it.

D. For us. For Paul and the Galatians, and for any who read the Galatian Epistle (Gal. 1:4; Eph. 5:2; Titus 2:14).

E. For me (Gal. 2:20). Can I not say, can you not say, can my neighbor not say, can everyone not say with Paul, "He gave Himself for me"?

II. He Gave Himself for What?

A. An offering and a sacrifice to God (see Eph. 5:2 and Heb. 9:14).

B. A ransom (a price—Matt. 20:28; Acts 20:28; 1 Cor. 6:19–20; 1 Tim. 2:6).

C. To redeem from all iniquity. To redeem means:

1. "To obtain at the market" (Rev. 5:9; 14:3–4).

2. "To obtain out of the market" (Gal. 3:13; 4:5).

3. "To loose by a price" (Titus 2:14; 1 Peter 1:18–19).

D. To purge (cleanse thoroughly) us from our sins (Titus 2:14; Heb. 1:3; 9:14; Rev. 1:5). Out and away go our sins like a dirty blotch of grease when pure gasoline is vigorously applied.

E. To deliver us from this present evil world (Gal. 1:4; Col. 1:13; 1 Thess. 1:10). This is a rescuing.

III. How Did God Give Himself?

A. Visibly. "This thing was not done in a corner." The whole universe looked upon this sight. "The people stood beholding" (Luke 23:35).

B. Valiantly. This was the giving of the strong Man (Heb. 2:14). "Bringing Satan to naught" (see Heb. 12:2–3).

C. Voluntarily. "He gave Himself" (John 10:17–18; Gal. 1:4).

D. Vicariously. "For our sins" (Gal. 1:4; 1 Peter 2:24).

E. Victoriously. "That He might deliver" (Gal. 1:4; Heb. 10:11–14).

John A. Ross

WITH ALL YOUR HEART

Seek the Lord (Deut. 4:29).

Serve the Lord (Deut. 10:12).

Love the Lord (Deut. 13:3).

Obey the Lord (Deut. 30:2).

Turn unto the Lord (Deut. 30:10).

Walk before the Lord (1 Kings 2:4).

Follow the Lord (1 Kings 14:8).

Praise the Lord (Ps. 86:12).

Trust the Lord (Prov. 3:5).

D. L. Moody